Moon Spells
for Witchcraft

*A Guide to Using the Lunar
Phases for Magic and Rituals*

Table of Contents

Introduction

Many people are drawn to the moon, and it's not surprising why. The moon is a powerful symbol of healing, transformation, mystery, and magic. It's been a vital force in human life for thousands of years, and it's no secret that the moon has always played an important role in witchcraft.

The moon has long been thought to strongly influence our minds and bodies. Many cultures look to the phases of the moon to determine their practices, from sacred rituals to everyday activities like farming. Today we still see evidence of the moon's influence in modern culture - consider how many aspects of our lives are ruled by "lunar calendars."

There is no doubt that the moon is steeped in magic, but how can you tap into this power yourself? This guide will show you the basics of Moon Spells for Witchcraft. It's an introduction to harnessing the lunar phases for magical purposes. The information in this book will lead you along a path of discovery and empowerment. As you learn about the moon, you will begin to see it as your ally and friend.

The first chapter covers the basics of Moon Spells for Witchcraft. It includes a brief history of moon worship and will help you identify your relationship with the moon. The second chapter is about the New Moon Rituals and Magic, where you will find information on when to cast your spells, what symbols to use, and how to charge your crystals. You will also discover a variety of New Moon Rituals for different uses.

The third chapter is about the Waxing Moon, where you will learn how to cast spells during this period. You'll get information on Candles and Oils and several spells you can cast with them. The fourth chapter covers the Magic of The Full Moon, where you will read about how to prepare for the full moon, cast spells during the full moon, and clean up after the full moon.

The fifth chapter discusses Waning Moon Spells, where you will learn about the waning moon and how to use it. You'll find information on cleansing, releasing, and reversing spells you have already cast. The sixth chapter talks about Moon Phases and Spells. Here, you will get information on the new, waxing, full, and waning moon phases and how they are taken advantage of. You will also get information on how to increase your psychic awareness and use it in your spells.

The seventh chapter is about Protection Spells. You will learn when to cast protection spells, what supplies you'll need, how to use them, and information about the types of protection spells you can cast. This book is designed for both novice practitioners who are new to magic and more advanced students of magic. Magic is about learning, growing, exploring, and evolving. There is always more to learn!

Moon Spells for Witchcraft is a concise introduction to the power of the moon. You will discover how this powerful ally can help you with your witchcraft and magical work. By the time you've finished reading this book, you will be ready to start casting spells of your own!

Chapter 1: Moon Spells for Beginners

The moon has been associated with magic for eons. People have studied the lunar cycle and sought its influence on the magic they were already practicing. The moon has been held in high regard throughout the world by different cultures. Throughout time, spellcasters have worked with the moon's phases. From simple spells for beginners to more complex rituals that can call upon the power of the full moon, you too will learn how to tap into the magic of the moon.

There are many ways to work with the moon's phases, and you will find that there are other books on the subject. You can adapt them to your style. You will find that some people do not cast spells during specific moon phases but instead consider the Moon to be the mother of all magic. It is said that she is the giver of life, love, and wisdom. She can be used to draw any type of energy to you, whether it is prosperity or psychic energy.

Working with the moon is a great way for beginners and experienced practitioners alike to learn about the moon's influence on magic. It is an easy way to get in touch with the lunar energies, and since the moon's influence is subtle, it can be a safe way to experiment with magic. With the information you will learn in this chapter, you can use Lunar Energy for simple spell casting purposes.

This chapter covers the basics of Moon spells for beginners. It includes a brief history of moon worship and will help you identify your relationship with the moon. This chapter explains how to perform a spell and what you can expect when performing magic. There is also a list of ingredients that most spells require and where you can find them.

Magical History of the Moon

For ages, the moon has been associated with magic and witchcraft. Many different cultures hold the moon in high regard. Before the invention of electricity, many people relied on the lunar cycle to live. The moon was used to measure time and provide a means to keep track of the days and months. As a result, people have been trying to understand the moon's power over nature for thousands of years.

There is no way to know which civilization or culture was the first to write about magic and the moon. Moon's association with magic goes back at least as far as the Paleolithic era. Evidence has been found of moon worship in the Neolithic period, during which it was common for magic to be used for hunting, healing, and fertility.

Hippocrates was a Greek physician known as the father of Western medicine. He believed that the phases of the moon affected a person's health and documented that a person's health is directly related to the seasons and climate. He also said that there is a correspondence between the phases of the moon and what a person may be suffering from.

It is also worth noting that the moon and earth share a gravitational connection. Both bodies exert an influence on tides. The moon affects how the weight of Earth-bound objects is distributed and how water flows on land and in the ocean.

The moon has been used as a symbol for different cultures and religions. In some traditions, the moon is a representation of female energy, goddesses, dark forces, or evil powers. It has also been associated with masculinity and male energy. For example, Norse mythology views the moon as the head of a male god Máni. Some cultures also saw it as a symbol of Mother Nature.

Your Relationship with the Moon

You may have a personal relationship with the moon. People who believe in astrology often have a bond with one of the zodiac signs, which are said to be ruled by different planets. Many witches, pagans, and Wiccans have a relationship with a particular deity representing a specific aspect of nature. You may also feel drawn to worshipping the moon because you sense that magic is more powerful during certain times of the month or night.

The way the moon affects you might depend on your relationship with it. For example: If you were born under the sign of Cancer, your zodiac ruling planet is the Moon. This connection might mean that you are more susceptible to the influence of the moon on your feelings, emotions, and mood. A relationship with the moon might also be tied to your personality type. To determine your compatibility with the moon, it is best to learn about each of its aspects.

You can determine your relationship with the moon through dream analysis. If you attempt to answer the question, "Why am I drawn to magic and moon spells?" you can expect an answer to surface in your dreams. If you are performing magic for a particular purpose, your subconscious mind may help you find the answer through the symbolism in your dreams.

Another way you can determine your relationship with the moon is to ask yourself these questions:

- Do I feel excited when the new moon appears?

- Do I have a strong connection to certain symbols of the moon?

- Do I feel more creative during certain nights of the month?

- Do dreams seem particularly vivid during the days of the full moon?

- Have I ever had a dream about the moon where it was central to the meaning of my message?

- Do I feel particularly introspective during the dark cycle of the moon?

- Do certain lunar aspects affect my personality?

If you have had any of these experiences, your relationship with the moon will likely be strong. The moon represents a powerful force of change and transformation. It is important to be aware of how it affects you and the kind of energy that might be present in the world when you are performing moon spells.

There is also a possibility that your connection to the moon will not seem significant. You might not feel as if the moon directly impacts your life, and you may be more influenced by other astrological factors. The moon can be a source of spiritual and magical inspiration, even if you do not think that it has the power to directly alter your life.

Moon Spells for Beginners

It is important to remember that a spell can be cast anytime, but moon spells are preferred during a full or waning moon. Depending on your magic's purpose and method, a dark moon is preferred for some spells and rituals. The best way to learn about spells is to experiment with seasonal magic. This type of spell casting involves using ingredients that are in season at a particular time of year. For example, if you are working with the magic of the fall season, it is best to use the leaves and fruits common during this time.

When working with moon spells for beginners, it is best to use simple and easy-to-find ingredients. The most common ingredients are listed below:

- Oil of your choice (olive oil is used to represent the moon)

- Salt or other water-absorbing crystals

- A chalice or other container for your spell

- White candles, a white candle holder, and matches or a lighter

- A dish for burning incense

When working with moon spells, it is important to remember that the most important aspect of spell work is "intent." If you intend to use magic as a method of transformation and connection, it will be effective. When performing your first few spells, choosing an area, you can practice in without any distractions is best.

A Basic White Moon Spell

Ingredients:

- A white candle and a candle holder.

- A chalice

- Anointed oil of your choice, preferably white

Procedure:

Step 1: Begin by cleansing yourself and the area around you. This can be done by using white sage or any other method you prefer

Step 2: Proceed to perform the Lesser Banishing Ritual of the Pentagram, especially if you are working indoors

Step3: Anoint your candle with anointed oil, and place it in the candle holder. Place the chalice of water near the candle, but not too close

Step 4: Light your candle and simply look at it without distraction

Step 5: When you feel the time has come, say a prayer to the Goddess and thank her for being with you

Step 6: Now, close your eyes and focus on the flame of the candle. Do not let anything distract you as you take three deep breaths. On the third breath, say a prayer asking for guidance and inspiration from the moon. Keep your eyes closed until you feel that you are done

Step 7: When you are ready, open your eyes and drink the water from the chalice

Note: If this is your first time performing a spell, do not expect immediate results. It may take several attempts before performing spells without distractions or difficulty.

If you would like to work with a particular phase of the moon, you will need to know what phase it is in and perform your spell accordingly. Moon phases change every day and typically last for about three days. You can find out what phase the moon is in by checking a calendar or the internet.

Moon Spell for Beginners: Love

Ingredients:

- A red or pink candle (red is preferred if you want to strengthen a relationship)

- Anointed oil of your choice

- A dish for burning incense or incense charcoal

Procedure:

Step 1: To begin, cleanse yourself and the area you will be working in

Step 2: Light the incense and allow it to burn for a few minutes

Step 3: Proceed to perform the Lesser Banishing Ritual of the Pentagram

Step 4: When you feel ready, anoint your candle with oil and place it in the candle holder

Step 5: Light your candle and focus on the flame. Say a prayer to Aphrodite or Selene in your mind and ask that they help you attract new love or strengthen your relationship with the one you already have

Step 6: When you feel that the time has come, close your eyes and focus on feeling the flame. Do not let anything distract you as you take three deep breaths. On the third breath, saying a prayer is asking for guidance and inspiration from Aphrodite or Selene

Step 7: When you are ready, open your eyes and say a prayer of thanks to either Aphrodite or Selene

Step 8: Now, extinguish your candle and wait until the next day to light it again with the same prayer

Moon Spell for Beginners: Money

Ingredients:

- A green candle (green is preferred if you want to attract money)

- Anointed oil of your choice

- A dish for burning incense or incense charcoal

Procedure:

Step 1: Repeat steps 1, 2, and 3 of the love spell

Step 2: When you feel ready, anoint your candle with anointed oil and place it in the candle holder

Step 3: Light your candle and focus on the flame. Say a prayer to Hermes or Hecate in your mind and ask that they help you attract new money or strengthen the flow of abundance in your life

Step 4: When you feel that the time has come, close your eyes and focus on feeling the flame. Do not let anything distract you as you take three deep breaths. On the third breath, saying a prayer is asking for guidance and inspiration from Hermes or Hecate

Step 5: When you are ready, open your eyes and say a prayer of thanks

Step 6: Now, extinguish your candle and wait until the next day to light it again with the same prayer. You can do this spell up to three times a day, but only once per phase of the moon

Moon spells are powerful and simple at the same time. If you have trouble with your spells, try using moon magic to strengthen it. Remember that the more energy you put into a spell, the more likely you will get results. Keep in mind that when doing spells for specific purposes, you should work with different phases of the moon to strengthen your intent. Keep a lunar calendar to help you plan out the best time to perform your spell. After completing a spell, you must always thank the moon to maintain a strong relationship with it.

Chapter 2: New Moon Rituals and Magic

One of the most popular types of spells is a new moon spell. The new moon is when there is no moon in the sky, and it happens every 28 days when the moon transitions from full to completely dark. Many people believe that such a time is ideal for magic because it is a great time for cleansing and purification.

A new moon ritual works best if you perform it on the day of the new moon itself. However, you can also do it until the end of the day after the new moon. This ritual can be done by itself, or you can pair it with another spell or ritual that has to do with healing, peace, love, or prosperity. The new moon only lasts one night and one day, so you'll want to perform this ritual during that brief period. This chapter focuses on the spells that are best performed when the moon is new. Besides that, the chapter includes what you can expect to achieve from those spells and how to cast them. It also includes advice on choosing the best spell for you and a list of ingredients that can be used when performing a new moon spell.

Types of New Moon Spells

There are many different types of new moon spells you can perform. You'll find a list on this page that includes some of the most popular spells that are best performed during a new moon. It also includes advice on how to choose the best type of spell for you, as well as a list of ingredients that can be used when performing a new moon spell.

Spell to Break Ties with Someone

If you want to break all ties with someone in your life, you'll need to perform a spell on the new moon. This is when you can expect to receive the most positive results because the time of a new moon is when you can expect things to be at their worst. This will make it easier for you to sever any ties you have with this person. This spell can be done for yourself, but it's often performed on behalf of someone else who wants to break ties with that person.

Ingredients:

- Black candle; the size of the candle depends on how long you want it to burn. It can be up to 3" in diameter

- Fireproof dish or cauldron; you can also use a fireplace if it's safe to do so

- Chalk; used to draw a circle around the dish

- Something to bind you and the other person together; it can be a string, an article of clothing, a photograph, or hair from each of you

Procedure:

Step 1: Cast a circle, and put an X on the floor with chalk. Stand in the circle and visualize whatever is holding you back from the person you want to break ties with

Step 2: Take the black candle, light it from a flame inside of a fireproof bowl or cauldron, and drip wax onto the X. As you do this, visualize the person being removed from your life as you continue to chant

"Let this connection be broken

Let them never again feel the desire to contact me"

Step 3: Allow the candle to burn in a safe place until it goes out on its own

Step 4: In the following days, you can expect this person to forget about you because there will be no emotional tie binding the two of you together

Love and Beauty Spells

If you like to perform spells that deal with love or beauty, the best time for you to do so is during a new moon. The next six days are also good times because Venus, the planet of love, rules them. If you want your spell to work well, focus on having a passionate and loving relationship with the person involved. If you need to, cast another spell on the next new moon so that your love and beauty spells will be empowered by each other.

As you can see, the new moon is a time of neutrality, so if you're looking for love spells that will not harm anyone involved, then the new moon is the best time for you. It's also a good day to begin things, so if you're looking for love, you might want to begin your search for a new moon. If you wait longer, the effects of your spell may wear off, and you'll have to repeat it for it to be effective.

Love spells may include but are not limited to spells for drawing love, binding a lover's heart and soul, protecting a current relationship, and removing obstacles from your path. Beauty spells may include but are not limited to spells for finding beauty, finding inner beauty, and developing a youthful appearance. Check out the list of ingredients to find those that can be useful when performing a beauty and love spell.

Ingredients:

- Bergamot, lavender, sandalwood, and red candle - used to draw love

- White candle and parchment paper with a lover's name written on it - used to bind a lover's heart and soul

- Red candle in a fireproof bowl or cauldron - used to light the above candle, can also be used by itself to draw love

Procedure:

Step 1: To draw love into your life, take a one-inch purple candle, drip wax onto a piece of parchment paper with the name of someone you'd like to attract written on it. Sprinkle the name with a blend of 14 drops of bergamot, 14 drops of lavender, and 14 drops of sandalwood. Wrap the paper around the candle so that it's firmly affixed to it, drip more wax onto the paper, and then light the candle. As you do this, visualize your love appearing in your life.

Step 2: If you're looking for a specific person, use a picture of them instead. Keep the picture on your altar next to the candle so that it's visible when you cast your circle. When you're done, allow the candle to burn out on its own.

Step 3: To bind a lover's heart and soul, take a new white candle and a piece of parchment paper with the name of your lover written on it. Light a red candle in a fireproof bowl or cauldron and drip wax onto the paper, and then chant:

"I bind your heart and soul to mine

So shall we never again be apart

So shall our hearts beat as one"

Step 4: Light the white candle and let it burn by itself. In the next new moon, you may expect love to come your way

Knowledge and Prosperity Spells

You can also perform spells that deal with knowledge or prosperity during a new moon. The next six days are again a good time for this. However, proceed with caution when performing spells that deal with knowledge or prosperity. This is because these spells can often lead to greed and materialism. That's why it's recommended to perform spells like this only when necessary and ensure that the spell doesn't become self-serving.

Spells for knowledge and prosperity can include but are not limited to finding a job, getting a promotion, and increasing your income. They can also include spells for attracting business success and wisdom, spells for adding wealth to your life, spells for gaining knowledge and wisdom, and spells to remove negative energy from your life. These spells can also help in increasing your intelligence, improving your memory, helping you make better decisions, and driving away bad ideas and thoughts.

Ingredients:

- Grey and black candle - used to attract prosperity

- Amethyst, dill seed, mint leaves, bay leaf, cloves, or anise seeds - used to increase your intelligence

- Gold candle, sandalwood incense, and frankincense resin - used to draw wealth

- A piece of rose quartz - used to drive away negative energy and bad ideas

Procedure:

Step 1: To attract prosperity, take a grey and black candle. Etch symbols of your desire on the gray candle for material gain, financial success, good luck, and wealth. As *you do this, chant:*

"As the wax drips down on me

So shall my desires for money and success come to be"

Step 2: Etch symbols on the black candle for authority and rank, power, and leadership. As you do this, chant:

"As the wax drips down on me

So shall my authority, power, and leadership increase"

Step 3: Light both candles, let them burn out on their own, and expect wealth to come your way

Choosing the Right Spell for You

There are many types of new moon spells that can be performed. However, it's best to choose a spell that suits your specific needs and what's most important to you. Some spells are easy, while others are more complex. So, you should choose a spell that matches your expertise and skill level. A spell is only as good as you make it.

You may want to begin by writing down all the problems you're currently experiencing. It may not be easy to do, but it will help you focus on the most important problems and how you can approach them. You may want to choose a spell that can cast away all your problems at once, but it's best to focus on one problem at a time.

The best way to choose a spell is by using your intuition. If a spell sounds right and feels right, go ahead, and perform it. However, don't be afraid to research the spell beforehand. You should also make sure that you understand the instructions correctly and know exactly what you're doing.

How to Perform a New Moon Ritual

Once you've chosen what type of spell to cast, it's time to prepare the ritual. There are many ways you can go about this. However, it's best to abide by the following steps.

1. Preparing for Your New Moon Ritual

When preparing for a new moon ritual, the first thing you should do is to purify the area. Cleansing your space will help you focus on what you're doing and keep bad energies away. You can cleanse the area by using sage, incense, or any other purification method you prefer.

2. Setting Your Intention

The next thing you need to do is set your intention. You should focus on why you're doing the ritual and what it is that you're trying to achieve. To do this, it's best to write your intention down. This will help you stay focused and ensure that the ritual is successful.

3. Starting Your New Moon Ritual

Pick an appropriate time and day for your new moon ritual. You should pick a specific window of time that you want to perform the ritual. This is because performing a new moon ritual at any time that's not within your designated window won't be as powerful as it could be. Make sure you pick a time and day where the moon is new.

4. Casting Your New Moon Spell

When it comes to casting your new moon spell, you should choose a particular corner of the area that you've chosen to perform your ritual in. If possible, try to face this corner while facing the new moon. You should then turn your back to the corner and perform your spell in its direction. This will help you make a connection and focus on the new moon.

5. How to End Your New Moon Ritual

Once you've finished performing your spell, it's time to end the ritual. You should deactivate your spell by saying something like, *"This ritual is over."* Then, you can thank any entities you've called for help. You may choose to blow them away, but this isn't necessary. Once you're done, it's time to clean up.

New moon rituals and magic can be performed to help you with your biggest problems. However, it's best to pick a spell that suits your needs and abilities. To ensure that the ritual is successful, it's best to set your intention, perform the ritual at the right time, and end it properly.

You will have a successful new moon ritual and magic experience by following the steps above. Once you've finished performing your spell, it's time to end the ritual. You should deactivate your spell by saying something like, *"This ritual is over."* Then, you can thank any entities that you've called for help. Once you're done, it's time to clean up.

Chapter 3: Waxing Moon

The Waxing Moon Phase is the first phase of the Moon Cycle. It follows the New Moon and precedes the Full Moon. In this phase, the moon will slowly become visible as it waxes from a thin crescent to a full circle in preparation for being reborn again at the next New Moon. During this phase, spells for growth are active and powerful because they draw forth energy towards something new. During this time, intentions can be carried into fruition with less effort than during the waning moon. Some traditions call the waxing moon "the Growing Moon."

The Waxing Moon is associated with new beginnings, birth, growth, success, and optimism. During this phase, one should focus on spells relating to self-improvement. It is a good time for planting new seeds, doing divination and magic involving love or romance. The Waxing Moon is also considered a good time for divination work. If you plan to do a reading or spell casting from a chart, it is best to do it during this phase of the moon cycle.

This chapter includes spells that can be used during the waxing moon and what you can expect to achieve with them. It includes advice on choosing a spell and a list of ingredients you can use during a waxing moon. The chapter also includes advice for performing spells during the nine nights of the waxing moon.

Waxing Moon Spells

Waxing Moon Spells are active spells with the intent to bring something new into your life, build upon what you have already achieved, or increase something. For example, you might be trying to increase your friendships, energy levels, income, or even your psychic abilities. The Waxing Moon is a good time to do magic for growth and development.

Waxing Moon spells should be cast during the Waxing Crescent Moon, up until the full moon. The Waxing Moon is considered a good time for divination and magic involving love or romance in many traditions. Waxing Moon spells and rituals can be done to celebrate and honor the deities of your tradition. If you are working with a particular deity, you might choose to do your spell work during their time of power (the New Moon, for Maiden Goddesses such as Artemis, Persephone, and Diana) or during the Waxing Crescent to increase your success.

The Waxing Crescent Moon is the best time for magic involving new beginnings, birth, growth, success, and optimism. For example, you could do a spell to increase your income or attract new clients at this time. You can also use it to help you stop procrastinating and start working on exciting new projects or to get unstuck. A Waxing Crescent Moon ritual can help you start over after a major change in your life, such as a graduation, divorce, or the loss of a loved one.

Nine Nights of the Waxing Moon

During each phase of the moon cycle, the energy is at its height during the night of that phase. Many traditions consider it to be most powerful to do spell work during the night of whatever phase the moon is in. This means that you can get the most from your magic by doing spells during the night of the Waxing Crescent Moon, the night of the First Quarter Moon, and so on.

During the Waxing Moon, you can celebrate nine nights of festivities. According to tradition, magical work is most powerful during the nine days leading up to the full moon. This is because you increase energy toward your goal with each passing day. You can work during the nine days of the Waxing Moon to celebrate the deities of your choosing.

During these nine nights, you can also perform magic to increase something or wish for something new in your life. For example, a businesswoman might do a spell to increase her income, or a new mother might perform a pregnancy blessing for a healthy birth. If you want something not harmful to anyone else, you should cast magic for it during the Waxing Moon.

Waxing Moon Phase Characteristics, Correspondences, and Amulets

The Waxing Moon is the growing phase of the moon cycle. It is also when you see the visible crescent shape of the moon before the First Quarter Moon. During this stage of the cycle, you can do spells for growth and rejuvenation. The Waxing Moon is ruled by the Maiden Goddess and the Young God. These deities also rule the cardinal signs of Aries, Cancer, Libra, and Capricorn. The element associated with this phase is air. Its planetary ruler is the planet Venus. Its colors are white, silver, and gold.

An amulet of the Maiden Goddess can be made from a crescent moonstone. Use it to empower your spells of growth and development. The appropriate stone is the heart-shaped moonstone if you do a spell for love. The Young God can be honored with amulets of sunstones. The appropriate stones are topaz and peridot when you perform magic for growth, fulfillment, and rejuvenation.

To work magic during the Waxing Moon, use a candle in color associated with this phase of the moon. Examples include white for new beginnings, green for growth, and silver for working with the Maiden Goddess. Several amulets can be helpful during a Waxing Moon spell. A waxing crescent moon pendant or earrings can be worn to empower your spells. During spell work, you might also wear a topaz ring or a peridot stone.

How to Cast a Waxing Moon Spell and Basic Spell Structure

One of the best ways to start a spell during the Waxing Moon is to think about what you want and put it into simple, positive wording. For example, if you want a raise at work, do not say something like, *"I want to get a pay increase."* Instead, try something positive like *"I am successful at work, and I get a raise."* This kind of wording helps you focus your mind on what you want without getting stuck on ideas of what you do not want.

The basic structure of a spell for the Waxing Moon follows this format:

Step 1: Decide what you want

Step 2: Prepare yourself for your spell. Take time to do whatever you need to do to center yourself and get ready

Step 3: Perform your spell work. This might include lighting candles, burning incense, and/or saying words of power or a spell written out in your own words

Step 4: Give thanks after performing the spell. This might include giving a small offering to the deities or the spirits

A waxing moon spell can be performed for any goal within the bounds of what is appropriate. Some example goals include money, love, and good health. You can also do magic to give yourself more energy or become better at a hobby. The appropriate time is during the Waxing Moon if you do a spell for love.

Types of Waxing Moon Spells

There are many types of spells that can be done during the Waxing Moon. Some examples include love spells, prosperity spells, money spells, healing spells, and growth spells. In general, you can cast a spell for any goal that fits with the power of the Waxing Moon. Some specific examples of spell work during the Waxing Moon include:

Money and Prosperity Spells

During the waxing moon, cast a spell for money and prosperity. This might include a spell where you visualize yourself as wealthy and prosperous or doing acts to attract money into your life.

Ingredients:

- 1 Green candle

- Paper and pen for writing your spell

- Dollar bill or another physical symbol of money (such as a coin)

- Frankincense resin, which can be burned as incense during spell work

Procedure:

Step 1: Decide what you want. This might include being able to pay your bills on time, having extra money for buying things that you need or want or attracting opportunities that can lead to money

Step 2: Prepare yourself for your spell. Take time to do whatever you need to do to center yourself and get ready

Step 3: Perform your spell work. Start by writing out your goal and then burning the paper in a green candle while visualizing yourself achieving your goal

Step 4: Give thanks after performing the spell. This might include giving a small offering to the deities or the spirits

Health and Healing Spells

You can work on healing ailments during the waxing moon. This might include doing spell work to heal physical illnesses or for getting better after surgery. You might also perform a spell to become healthier or to feel better.

Ingredients:

- White candle

- Any herbs that are associated with health

- Paper and pen for writing your spell

- A small stone that represents health, such as a peridot stone

- Chamomile flowers, which can be burned as incense during spell work

Procedure:

Step 1: Decide what you want. This might include being healthy, recovering from an illness or injury, healing someone else who is sick, or feeling stronger and healthier

Step 2: Start by preparing yourself for your spell. Cleanse your area and light some incense while taking time to center yourself

Step 3: Perform your spell work. Write out your goal on a piece of paper and then burn it in a white candle. Visualize yourself being healthy as you burn the paper

Step 4: Give thanks after performing the spell. This might include giving a small offering to the deities or the spirits

Luck Spell

If you need a protection spell, do it during the waxing moon, because it is associated with both new beginnings and strength. Using a white candle is recommended for any spell for protection.

In addition to the four elements of witchcraft, there are also five directions you can work with during a spell. The four elements correspond to the cardinal directions of north, south, east, and west, while the fifth direction is up. Working with the five directions can greatly expand your spell work and add a lot of power to magic.

Ingredients:

- 1 Peach candle

- Paper and pen for writing your spell

- Sage leaves or another herb that represents the upper direction

- Cinnamon chips, which can be burned as incense during spell work

Procedure:

Step 1: Decide what you want. This might include protection, luck, or gaining more power in your life

Step 2: Start by preparing yourself. Cleanse your area and light some incense while taking time to center yourself

Step 3: Perform your spell work. Write down your goal on a piece of paper and then burn it in a peach candle while visualizing yourself achieving your goal

Step 4: Give thanks after performing the spell. This might include giving a small offering to the deities or the spirits

The waxing moon is a great time for spell work because it's when it's growing. Spells done during this period are said to bear the best results. The waxing moon is also a time for growth, including working toward future goals and feeling better. People who turn to the waxing moon for magical energy typically focus on success, health, and protection. However, many other areas of life can be enhanced during this time.

The best way to use the waxing moon is to decide what you want and then work toward that goal. You can also tie your spell work into any goal you have for the entire year. For example, if your goal is to get into a new relationship, you might enhance this desire by doing spell work for love. This can include improving your self-esteem, getting out of the house more often, and making yourself more attractive to potential partners.

Some people find it easier to work with the moon in terms of phases, but others prefer to work with the waxing and waning periods. There is no right or wrong way to work with the moon, so you should choose whichever option feels best. It's recommended that you use both phases for the best results.

Chapter 4: The Magic of the Full Moon

Witches, magicians, and spellcasters of every kind have always been enamored with the moon. In fact, in many pagan religions, the moon is considered a deity in its own right, female by nature and associated with good fortune. The full moon is the optimum time to perform any spell that has to do with luck, happiness, love, health, and peace. Psychic abilities and intuition are also heightened at this time. The magic of the full moon is powerful. If you are into witchcraft, the power that comes from the full moon can be harnessed in your spells. The full moon is the center of all things regarding witchcraft and other forms of divination.

The full moon represents the height of power. It is a time to perform the most difficult spells and workings because it holds the most power when the moon is at its fullest. This is why you should only perform spells during this time. This chapter includes spells that can be used during the full moon and what you can expect to achieve with them. It also includes advice on choosing a spell and the ingredients you can use during a full moon. The chapter also includes advice for performing spells on the night of the full moon and throughout its entirety.

Full Moon Spell Basics

Before you perform any spell, you should know what to expect. If you cannot produce the desired results, you are likely doing something wrong. For example, if your spell promises to attract love, but you fail to do so for two months in a row, it might be time to find out what you are doing wrong. Spells do not always work on the first try, so you must keep trying until your desired result is achieved. Examine what you are doing wrong and try to fix it before moving on to another spell.

Many people think that the full moon is only good for attracting love, money, and other material things. However, this is not true. Many spells can be performed during the full moon, which has nothing to do with attracting anything material. Think of spells as a way to tell the universe what you want. The full moon is simply a time when your spell will be stronger than usual.

The most popular spells that can be performed during the full moon are love, money, and protection spells. These are not the only types of spells you can do, but they are the most common. If there is a specific type of spell that you would like to perform during the full moon, you can do so even if it is not one of the three types mentioned. There are many spells that deal with other things such as psychic powers, luck at games of chance, astral projection, dream spells, etc.

Spells for Psychic Abilities and Intuition

Moon spells for psychic abilities and intuition increase your ability to feel what others think. An increased ability to feel what others are thinking at this time of the month is often called "the gift." It is also not uncommon for people who use this ability to become more empathetic. This innate sense of empathy is what makes spells for psychic abilities different from other types of spells. The most common moon spells for psychic abilities are related to love. Using these spells will help you figure out if a certain person is right for you before you take things to the next level.

Ingredients:

- A cup of chamomile tea

- A good book

- A pen and paper

- Your favorite comfy blanket or throws

- An open mind

Procedure:

Step 1: Make your cup of chamomile tea by boiling some water in a medium-sized pot and throwing in some chamomile flowers. Once the water starts to boil, turn off the stove and allow it to sit for a few minutes. Then, pour the water into a cup and add a teaspoon of honey. Stir until everything is mixed well, and enjoy your favorite book with the hot cup of tea in your hands.

Step 2: The next step is very important. Relax and allow the tea to work its magic while you enjoy your book. You should not think about anything in particular. If you are self-conscious about wasting time or if you feel obligated to do something specific, this spell will not work. You need to relax, and your mind needs to be empty of any thoughts for the spell to work.

Step 3: Once you feel like you are all relaxed, pick up your pen and paper. Concentrate on what you want to know about the person who interests you. It could be something simple like whether you should go on a date with them or something more complex such as who they are deep down. Write down whatever comes to mind, and do not judge your thoughts at all.

Step 4: When you feel like you have done enough, say a little chant to yourself, such as *"I now know everything I need to know."* This will end the spell, and everything you wrote down should be revealed to you.

Destiny Spells

Destiny spells are those that will give you your heart's desire. This type of spell is often the most difficult to perform because it involves asking for things you can't be sure about. If a person performs a love spell and asks for a specific type of partner, it is pretty clear whether or not they will get what they want. Destiny spells don't work like this. They ask for the most amazing things and hope they will happen.

Ingredients:

- A red candle

- Honey

- Cinnamon powder

- Nutmeg powder

- A mortar and pestle

- A piece of parchment paper

Procedure:

Step 1: Light the red candle to get your heart's desire

Step 2: While the candle is still burning, grind up the cinnamon and nutmeg in the mortar and pestle

Step 3: Next, drip honey onto the cinnamon and nutmeg powder until it forms a thick paste. Spread the resulting mixture onto the parchment paper

Step 4: Allow the candle to continue burning until it goes out by itself. Then, press your thumb into the paste and lift it to reveal your destiny

Healing Spells

Healing spells are a common type of moon spell because pretty much everyone has been sick at one point or another. There is no denying the power of a moon magic spell when it comes to getting rid of something causing you physical discomfort. It is worth noting that many of these spells also double as wish spells.

Ingredients:

- 2 Tablespoons of dried chamomile flowers

- 1 Tablespoon of dried lavender flowers

- 1 Tablespoon of dried peppermint leaves

- A piece of paper or a photo of yourself

- A small bowl

- Olive oil or plain yogurt

Procedure:

Step 1: Using the mortar and pestle, grind up the dried chamomile, lavender, and peppermint leaves

Step 2: Next, mix in a bit of olive oil or yogurt until you achieve a consistency like thick paint

Step 3: If you are using an image, place it in the middle of the paper. Next to it, write your name and what you want

Step 4: Now, take the mixture and place it on top of the image or paper. Dot it around the edges with your fingers until a decent amount is covering the affected area

Step 5: Place the bowl over the affected area and chant your intention out loud

Step 6: Finally, remove the bowl and allow the mixture to dry. Then, crumble it up and burn it

Positive Energy Spells

Positive energy spells are uplifting moon spells that can improve your physical or emotional state. They are the most difficult of the full moon spells because positive energy is something we all create in our lives. It can be very difficult to control, and it spreads in interesting and sometimes unpredictable ways. Be sure to put just as much attention into casting this spell as you would any other.

- **Ingredients:** An orange candle

- A bowl of sea salt

- Frankincense or sandalwood essential oil

Procedure:

Step 1: Light the orange candle to get rid of all negative energy in your life

Step 2: While the candle is still burning, take the bowl of sea salt and move it counterclockwise around your body

Step 3: Continue this process for about 10 minutes

Step 4: Finally, place the bowl of sea salt on your altar or somewhere safe where it can go undisturbed. Allow the candle to burn out on its own

Banishing Spells

Banishing spells are moon spells that can be cast to prevent something bad from coming into your life. They are great for warding off the proverbial dark clouds that dampen the light of your day. It is important to remember that you can banish anything with these spells, even positive things. So, approach this subject in a manner that makes the most sense to you.

Ingredients:

- A black candle

- Black tea or black coffee

- A piece of parchment paper

Procedure:

Step 1: Light the black candle to protect yourself from whatever you feel is a negative influence in your life

Step 2: Next, take a small amount of the black tea or coffee and use it to draw a banishing pentagram on the piece of parchment paper

Step 3: Once the pentagram is drawn, chant your intention over it

Step 4: Finally, set the parchment paper on fire and allow the candle to burn out

Prosperity and Abundance Spells

This type of moon spell is designed to bring more money into your life or enhance your ability to attract financial opportunities. Prosperity spells can be cast using a variety of different ingredients, and they are known for being very potent. There is usually a financial risk to these kinds of spells, though some witches believe that if you have done everything in your power to obtain prosperity on your own, then it is okay to use magic.

Ingredients:

- A green candle

- A bowl of fresh water

- Asparagus, basil, or mint leaves

Procedure:

Step 1: Light the green candle and place it in a spot where it is unlikely to tip over or cause anything to catch fire

Step 2: Next, take the bowl of fresh water and place it on your altar or somewhere safe where it can go undisturbed

Step 3: When you are ready, place the bowl of fresh water next to the candle and sprinkle in your herbs

Step 4: Chant your intention over the mixture

Step 5: Finally, place the bowl of saltwater on your altar or somewhere safe where it can go undisturbed. Allow the candle to burn out on its own

Advice for Working with the Full Moon

The full moon is known for its significance in the realm of spells and witchcraft. It acts as a sort of compass for helping you find a spiritual foothold in a sometimes uncertain world. During a full moon, there are several things you can do to make the most of this spiritual energy:

- Perform moon magic on the night of the full moon

- Perform moon magic during the entire time the full moon is in effect

- Perform any ritual or spell on the night of the full moon that you would like to see come to fruition

- Perform any ritual or spell during the entire five days the full moon is in effect

- Recharge items meant for moon magic or witchcraft

Moon spells can be used for just about anything. They are great because the moon itself has such a strong effect on all living things. If you are looking to make more of an impact with your magic, then choosing a spell designed to be cast on the night of the full moon can be just the thing you need. Moon spells are great because they create a distinctive spiritual energy that is hard to find anywhere else. Have fun with these spells, and remember that you can cast any spell at all during a full moon.

Chapter 5: Waning Moon

Waning Moon spells are best performed when the Moon is getting smaller and is, therefore, its weakest. The first quarter, or waxing moon, occurs when the Moon increases in size from a new moon. The Full Moon occurs when the Moon is full and reaches its peak. The third quarter, or waning moon, occurs when a full moon decreases in size until it becomes a new moon again.

The Waning Moon's energy works well for banishing and removing things from your life. This includes bad habits, bad luck, and negative energies that may be holding you back. This can also be a good time to do spells to remove obstacles in your way. This can be a very good time to cast spells for removing things from your life that you no longer want. It can also be used to remove bad habits and bad luck from your life. However, the waning moon's energy does not work well for gaining things or attracting things into your life.

This chapter is for those who want to focus on banishing, releasing, and letting go. This chapter explores spells that can be used during the waning moon and what you can expect to achieve with them. It also includes advice on choosing a spell and the ingredients you can use during a waning moon. The chapter also includes advice for performing spells during the nine nights of the third quarter and throughout its entirety.

How to Choose a Spell

Choosing a spell can be difficult. To choose the right spell for you, it's recommended you start by asking yourself what you are looking for. This will help you determine what sort of spell you should do. For example, if you are looking to remove something from your life, then a spell to banish things from your life would be the best choice. If you want to gain something, then a spell for attraction or increase would be the best choice.

Several types of spells can be used during the waning moon. Some examples of these spells include:

- Remove bad habits or addictions

- Remove a curse placed on you or someone else

- Release a spirit from a haunted place

- Release pent-up emotions, old memories, or bad experiences

- Convert negative energy into positive energy

- Banish something from your life

- Remove obstacles in your way

- Release a spirit from this world and into the next

- Release excess baggage

What to Expect When You Cast a Spell

Expect the unexpected when you do a spell. The results of spells are not always what we expect them to be because we, as humans, often try to understand the un-understandable. Sometimes, there's a disconnect between what we can understand and what can be done. This is because magic simply does not work the way we think it would. We try to fit what we know into what we don't know.

When you cast a spell, the best thing to do is to let go of expectations and accept the possibilities. We expect things to happen, but we don't know exactly how they will manifest. We just need to let go and let it happen. This way, we can benefit from the possibilities and not fight against them.

Spells for the Waning Moon

During the waning moon, it's best to do spells that banish bad habits, release bad luck or negative energy, remove obstacles in your way, and remove things from your life. You can also do spells for releasing, converting, and banishing.

The best times to do these spells are when you see the moon wane. However, there are several other times during a third-quarter moon that you can do spells and perform rituals:

- The day of the new moon

- Nine nights after the new moon (inclusive)

- The night before the full moon (inclusive)

- The day after the full moon (exclusive)

The following spells can be performed during a third-quarter moon. This means you can do them nine nights after the new moon, following the full moon, or the day before the next new moon.

Spell to Banish Bad Habits

Ingredients:

- 1 White candle

- Matches or lighter

- 2 Tablespoons of dirt (or ashes) from the fireplace/hearth

- 1 Tablespoon of salt

- 9" Square of white or beige cloth

Procedure:

Step 1: Place the dirt on the cloth and fold the corners of the cloth together to make a small package

Step 2: The dirt represents your bad habit or addiction, so take it and wrap it in the cloth until all you can see is the dirt

Step 3: Place this package beneath your bed or in a place where you will not see it

Step 4: Light the white candle and say a chant to release your bad habit or addiction into the earth. Chant:

"This bad habit (or addiction) is now part of the earth. It shall remain there for nine days and will soon be gone from my life. So, mote it be."

Step 5: Blow out the candle and say, *"With harm to none, so mote it be."*

Spell to Banish a Curse

Ingredients:

- White or blue candle

- Salt

Procedure:

Step 1: If you know who cast the curse on you, or if there's a name attached to it, place that person's name and any pertinent information for this spell on a piece of paper and burn it in your cauldron or in a fireproof container.

Step 2: Once the candle is lit, place the salt in your hand and say, *"Salt is what keeps me pure. I cleansed myself with salt to rid myself of this curse, so mote it be."*

Step 3: Light the candle and say, *"All curses are now gone from my life. So, mote it be."*

Step 4: Blow out the candle and say, *"With harm to none, so mote it be."*

Spell to Remove Negative Energy

Ingredients:

- Red or pink candle

- 1 Tablespoon of sea salt

- 1 Tablespoon of fresh lemon juice

Procedure:

Step 1: Pour the salt into a bowl

Step 2: Add some lemon juice and mix it with your fingers until you create a paste

Step 3: Create a design or symbol on the candle with the mixture

Step 4: Light the candle and say, *"I banish negative energy from my life. I am rid of all evil and harm to none."*

Step 5: Blow out the candle and say, *"With harm to none, so mote it be."*

Spell to Remove Obstacles

Ingredients:

- Red or pink candle

- 1 Tablespoon of olive oil

- 1 Tablespoon of vinegar

- 1 Tablespoon of sea salt

Procedure:

Step 1: Add the salt to the oil and mix them

Step 2: Do the same with the vinegar and oil until you create a paste

Step 3: Create a design or symbol on the candle with the mixture

Step 4: Light the candle and say, *"I banish all obstacles of my life. I am rid of all evil and harm to none."*

Step 5: Blow out the candle and say, *"With harm to none, so mote it be."*

Spell to Remove Negative Thoughts

Ingredients:

- Red or pink candle

- Blood orange essential oil

- 1 Tablespoon of dried thyme leaves

Procedure:

Step 1: Place the thyme and the oil in a bowl.

Step 2: Mix them until you create a paste.

Step 3: Create a design or symbol on the candle with the mixture.

Step 4: Light the candle and say, *"I banish all negative thoughts from my life. I am rid of all evil and harm to none."*

Step 5: Blow out the candle and say, *"With harm to none, so mote it be."*

Spell to Manifest Your Desires into Reality

Ingredients:

- Nine locks of your hair. (You can use other people's hair, but they must consent to that first)

- Brown, white, and black candles

- Small bowl

- White thread

Procedure:

Step 1: Add the hair to the bowl.

Step 2: Add some salt and say, *"Salt is what keeps me pure. I cleansed myself with this salt for this spell, so mote it be."*

Step 3: Mix the hair with salt and thread until you create a ball.

Step 4: Light the brown candle and say, *"This is my will. I am ready to release this spell into the universe."*

Step 5: Light the white candle and say, *"What I need is already within me. It has been from the start."*

Step 6: Light the black candle and say, *"I ask for my desires to come to me. I am ready."*

Step 7: Hold the ball in your hands and say, *"I release all insecurities. I give thanks for my success."*

Step 8: Toss the ball behind you outside of your house and say, *"This spell is now set into motion. So, mote it be."*

Spell to Heal a Broken Heart

Ingredients:

- 9 White candles. (You can use red candles if you prefer)

Procedure:

Step 1: Place the candles in a circle and light each one

Step 2: While lighting each candle, say, *"Healing light for me. Healing energy surrounds me. Healing light for [person's name] and their heart."*

Step 3: Leave the candles lit until they completely burn out. This spell is not complete until the last candle has burned out

How to Perform a Spell During the Nine Nights of the Third Quarter

During the nine nights of the third quarter, you can work on a spell every night. Work with one goal each night or work on different spells each night. If you're working with a group, you can guide them in performing spells every night. The only rule here is that each spell must be different. When working with the group, you can do a spell for protection on one night, a prosperity spell on another night, and so forth. If you are working by yourself, feel free to do whatever you want during these nine nights. Rituals and spells can be done for whatever your heart desires. You may want to focus on healing or resolving conflict with family members, or you might want to try working on a new money spell. Let your heart be your guide for this period.

Night 1: Protect yourself and your home from outside influences

Night 2: Protection of the self and one's possessions

Night 3: Protection from deception and manipulation

Night 4: Protection from physical danger

Night 5: Make a wish come true

Night 6: Increase of popularity

Night 7: Good fortune

Night 8: Abundance in all things

Night 9: All that you have worked for will come to fruition

The nine nights of the third quarter are perfect for spells that stop outside influences, protection, and anything that has to do with strength. Most spells are designed to bring you protection from negative outside influences or dangers. Many people choose this time to make wishes come true or increase their popularity. If you are looking to bring in good fortune or protect your home, then the nine nights of the third quarter are perfect for you.

If you find yourself performing a spell during the nine nights of the third quarter and you notice that your wish does not come true, then it is not a mistake. It only means you are supposed to make your way or take it into your own hands to make your wish come true. The same goes if you feel like you are in physical danger, your spell is to make sure that harm does not come to you. If the danger is already there, your spell ensures that it does not become bigger and cause even more harm.

Let your instincts guide you when working with the nine nights of the third quarter and your spells. If it feels right, go for it. If you find that you are being pulled in a different direction, follow your instincts, and go where they lead you.

The waning moon is the time to give thanks for all you have in your life. It is also a great time to let go of the things that are not good for you or your well-being. When you combine the magic of the waning moon with spells, you can work on banishing, releasing, and letting go. You can also fight off outside influences that are trying to harm you and your loved ones. If working with a group, then the waning moon is perfect for spells that work on community, friendship, and love. When working by yourself, the waning moon is excellent for personal goals, growth, and moving forward. You can do so many things with the waning moon, but always remember tolet your instincts guide you when performing magic.

Chapter 6: Moon Phases for Magic and Rituals

The moon is one of the most powerful natural tools for magic and rituals. The stages of the moon and their meanings offer a wealth of information to those who study them. Moon phases are a great way to plan magic spells. Knowing the phases of the Moon can help you find the right timing for lunar rituals and magic. But what are the moon phases? How can they help your magic and rituals? This chapter explains the moon's cycle, which can easily be applied to spells. This chapter explains how the moon's cycle can affect different types of magic. There is also advice on choosing a spell based on the moon's cycle and a list of ingredients that can be used during different parts of the moon's cycle. There is also information on how to perform a spell during each part of the moon's cycle.

The moon phases are when the moon passes through its phases according to the sun, forming a natural cycle. The moon cycles are also linked to women's menstrual cycle, and they are strongly associated with women, fertility, birth, and death. Therefore, it is not surprising that the moon is one of the main elements used in magic and witchcraft practices.

The Moon Phases and Their Meanings

There are eight main stages of the lunar cycle, each with its own meaning. These stages are commonly referred to as new moon, waxing crescent, first quarter, waxing gibbous, full moon, waning gibbous, third quarter, and waning crescent. Each of these phases has its importance and meaning to people who practice the craft. Unlike some other occult topics, there are no hard and fast guidelines for when to work magic with the phases of the Moon. Each person's psychic sensitivity and relationship with the Moon are different. Some people do their best magic on the New Moon, while others prefer to work on a Full Moon. The best advice is to experiment to find which phase of the Moon is most conducive for your purposes.

The phases of the moon have long been associated with magic, rituals, and spell casting. Many witches are aware that certain lunar phases are more favorable for magic and spell casting than others, but it is also important to be aware of the different energies that each phase offers. As you probably know, the moon goes through its phases in a predictable cycle, from new to full and back again. This cycle repeats itself approximately every twenty-nine days or one month. Each of these phases has its special energy that the witch can harness.

Phase 1: New Moon

The New Moon is an important time to perform magic, as well as to begin new projects. This phase of the moon begins when the moon cannot be seen at all. From the perspective of the earth, it looks like the moon is not even there. It may be difficult to see the moon at all during this time, but that does not mean that it is not there.

New Moons are perfect for new projects and beginnings. If you're starting a new project or goal, you should wait until the phase of the New Moon to begin. This way, as soon as you start (at the exact time of the New Moon), your project will stay strong for twenty-eight days.

New Moons are also good times to perform magic for something you wish to send into the future (and it is also a good time to begin doing divination). The New Moon is a better time to do spells for birth, endings, and beginnings.

The New Moon is an excellent time to plant seeds for future growth. This is a great time to do candle magic and to make wishes and prayers.

The New Moon is also good for empathy spells (working with spirits, specifically the Otherworld).

Phase 2: Waxing Crescent Moon

The Waxing Crescent Moon begins after the New Moon has passed and is characterized by the first tiny sliver that we see in the sky at night. The Waxing Crescent Moon continues to become more and more visible each night. This phase is the best time to do magic for growth, health, prosperity, and any other project that relies on steady progress.

This phase of the Moon is good for spells to increase personal power, money, love, or sex. It is also a good time to do magic to help someone recover from illness.

The Waxing Crescent Moon is also a good time to do divination work with Tarot cards, runes, or other means of divination.

It is also a good time to do magic to help you see into the future, travel in your astral body, or contact departed loved ones.

The Waxing Crescent Moon is a good time to do spells involving the element of water and magic that involves healing yourself.

Phase 3: First Quarter Moon

The First Quarter Moon occurs when exactly half of the moon's surface is visible. This phase is good for spells involving air, logic, communication, and ideas.

This phase of the moon is also good for magic involving justice, legal matters, and politics. It is also a good time to begin new projects that involve strength or asserting yourself.

This phase of the moon is good for divining information about the past, present, or future. It is also a good time to begin new projects involving the element of fire.

Phase 4: Waxing Gibbous Moon

The Waxing Gibbous Moon begins when more than half of the moon's surfaces are visible. This phase is good for magic involving the element of earth, material things, grounding your energy, and keeping yourself safely rooted in reality.

This phase of the moon is good for spells to improve memory or studying. It is also a good time to begin new projects that involve construction or building.

The Waxing Gibbous Moon is a good time to do magic that involves increasing abundance, prosperity, wealth, or luck.

This phase of the moon is good for magic that involves animals, fertility, or pregnancy. It is also a good time to begin projects involving practicality or taking care of yourself.

Phase 5: Full Moon

The Full Moon is when the entire visible surface of the moon is lit up by the sun. This phase is good for magic involving the element of fire, passion, sex, fertility, and creativity.

The Full Moon is a good time to work magic involving communication, inspiration, confidence, willpower, overcoming obstacles, and breaking free.

This phase of the moon is good for magic that involves transformation, rebirth, or renewal. It is also a good time to begin projects that involve expansion or bringing something into being.

The Full Moon is a good time to do spells involving elemental magic. It is also a good time for divination and psychic development, as the

Full Moon is a time when the veil between our world and other worlds is thin.

Phase 6: Waning Gibbous Moon

The Waning Gibbous Moon begins when more than half of the moon's surface is lit up by the sun but less than the entire visible surface. This phase is good for magic involving the element of water.

This phase of the Moon is good for spells that involve friendship and harmony with others. It is also a good time to begin teamwork projects or work with others.

The Waning Gibbous Moon is a good time for magic that involves sensuality, comfort, trust in yourself and others, or seeing the good in others.

This phase of the moon is also a good time for magic that involves the element of earth or changes involving material things. It is also a good time for divination work with Tarot cards, runes, or other means of divination.

Phase 7: Third Quarter Moon

The Third Quarter Moon occurs when exactly half of the moon's surface is visible. This phase is good for magic involving the element of air or using your mind to solve problems.

This phase of the moon is good for magic involving the element of fire or using your creative energies. It is also a good time to begin projects involving ambition, motivation, new ideas, and innovation.

The Third Quarter Moon is a good time for magic involving water or emotions, love, and sexuality. It is also a good time to begin projects involving intuition, dreams, and visions.

This phase of the moon is a good time for magic that involves physical energy, sex, passion, or action. It is also a good time to begin projects involving strength or asserting yourself.

Phase 8: Waning Crescent Moon

The Waning Crescent Moon begins when the moon's visible surface is just barely illuminated. This phase is a time of magic involving the element of water and your unconscious mind, so it is best used for divination or meditation.

This phase of the moon is good for magic that involves new beginnings, positive change, or cleansing. It is also a good time to begin projects that involve healing or helping others.

The Waning Crescent Moon is a good time for magic involving earth, friendship, and harmony.

It is also a good time to begin teamwork projects or work with others.

This phase of the moon is good for magic that involves physical energy, sex, passion, or action. It is also a good time to begin projects involving strength or asserting yourself.

Phase 9: Dark Moon

The Dark Moon occurs when the moon is not visible in the sky. This phase is still used for magic involving the element of earth, but it is only used for advanced spellcasters. It's best not to attempt Dark Moon magic until you have worked with the moon's other phases several times.

How to Choose a Spell

When choosing a spell from this book, first determine what kind of moon phase you are in. You can match spells to the appropriate moon phase and the corresponding energy and type of magic it will work best for. For example:

- A spell involving new beginnings, positive change, or cleansing could be done during the Waning Crescent Moon.

- A spell involving sensuality, comfort, or trusting others could be done during the Full Moon.

- A spell involving healing or helping others could be done during the Waning Gibbous Moon.

- A spell involving ambition, motivation, new ideas, and innovation could be done during the Waxing Gibbous Moon.

- A spell involving intuition, dreams, or visions could be done during the Waning Crescent Moon.

Most Common Ingredients for Moon Magic

The following ingredients are some of the most commonly used in magic spells. If you are unsure what ingredient to use for a particular spell, these are good choices.

- **Allspice**: For luck, attracting good fortune

- **Almond Oil**: For love and romance

- **Apple:** For healing, fertility, and prosperity

- **Basil:** For purification, exorcism, or protection

- **Bay Leaves**: For protection and exorcism

- **Boneset:** For healing, exorcism, and protection

- **Caraway Seeds:** To attract money, luck, and prosperity

- **Carnation Petals:** For unconditional love

- **Cinnamon:** For purification, prosperity, and lust

- **Cloves:** For purification, exorcism, and protection

- **Coconut:** For stability and security in a situation

- **Cumin Seeds:** For attracting money, luck, and prosperity

- **Devil's Claw:** For purification or exorcism.

- **Dill Seeds:** For protection, peace, and exorcism

- **Dragon's Blood:** For purification, protection, and strength

- **Eucalyptus Leaves:** For healing, purification, and exorcism

- **Fennel Seeds**: For protection, love, and sleep

- **Fig:** For fertility and protection

- **Frankincense:** For purification, strength, and protection

- **Garlic:** For protection and exorcism

- **Ginger:** For lust, courage, and exorcism

- **High John Root:** For luck in gambling or games of chance

- **Honeysuckle:** For divination and love

- **Hyssop:** For purification, exorcism, and protection

- **Jasmine Flowers**: For love, fertility, and divination

- **Juniper Berries:** To purify or exorcise a location, prevent a psychic attack, or drive off a rival

- **Lavender**: For psychic power, protection, purification, and love

- **Lemon Peel**: To attract money, luck, and prosperity

- **Lemongrass**: For purification, exorcism, and protection

- **Licorice Root:** For money and protection

- **Mace**: For exorcism and to undo a hex or break a curse

- **Magnolia Leaves:** For divination and love

- **Mint:** For purification, healing, exorcism, money rituals, and lust

- **Nutmeg:** To attract good luck and money

- **Olive Oil:** For healing, purification, protection, and love

- **Patchouli:** For lust, love, and exorcism

- **Peppermint:** For purification, love, healing, luck, money rituals, psychic power, protection, lust, and exorcism

- **Pine Needles**: For protection, purification, exorcism, and healing

- **Rose Petals:** For love, divination, and purification

- **Rosemary:** For purification, love, health, money rituals, protection, psychic power, and exorcism

- **Sage:** For purification, protection, and healing

- **Sandalwood:** For divination and love

- **Spearmint:** For money, purification, love, and lust

- **Sunflower Petals:** For fertility and protection

- **Sweetgrass:** For purification, protection, and exorcism

- **Yarrow Flowers:** To prevent psychic attacks or drive off rivals

- **Wormwood:** For divination, protection, and preventing psychic attacks

The moon's cycle is one of the most important natural cycles for spells. Knowing which spell to pick during each part of the moon's cycle can be a big help when selecting a spell. As you can see, every phase of the moon has a different type of magic associated with it. If you are wondering what type of magic to use for a particular spell, look at the phase of the moon. While the list I have given you is not all-inclusive, it gives you a starting point and covers some of the most common types of spells.

Chapter 7: Protection Spells

The full moon's energy is ideal for protection spells, banishing spells, and cleansing rituals. If you have a strong need for protection, this is a good time to cast a spell that will protect you, your home, and your loved ones. Trying to cleanse yourself or your home during a full moon can also help you achieve success with these magic rituals. The power of the full moon will pull negative energies out of your body and away from your home.

It is important to protect yourself from negative energy and other people trying to manipulate you when performing magic. Protection spells are a good way of blocking out negative energy, but they can also be used to protect yourself from other people trying to manipulate you. This chapter includes a list of ingredients you can use for protection spells, advice on choosing the best spell for you, and tips for performing a successful protection spell.

Ingredients for Protection Spells

The following common ingredients will be beneficial for your protection spells:

Athame - An athame is often used in magic rituals because of its ability to focus energy. The black handle on your athame should be made from a material special to you.

Cauldron - This is a very powerful source of energy that can be used to burn protective herbs and resins. The fire under the cauldron will heat your special protection oil, which you can then use to anoint the doorways and windows of your home.

Broom - A broom is a tool that can be used to cleanse your ritual area from negative energy.

Black Salt - This is created by burning salt and grounding it up into a fine powder. The ground black salt can be used to anoint doorways, windows, and other areas of your home that are susceptible to negative energy.

Garlic - This ingredient has long been used to protect people against evil spirits. Garlic can be added to your protective bath water or hung around your neck to provide protection when you are venturing out of your home.

Jet - This is a protective stone with an ebony color. Jet can also be used to make an athame, and it sharpens the senses of your mind.

Cinnamon - In some traditions, cinnamon and/or frankincense is burned to create protective smoke.

Rosemary - This herb has long been used for protection and purification. It can be added to your bath water or written on a piece of paper and hung in places where you spend a lot of time.

Frankincense - This herb can also be burned to create protective smoke.

Sage - Burning this herb will result in the creation of a protective smoke.

Cedar - This is another herb with which you can create a protective smoke.

Protective Herbs

When performing a protection spell, you can choose ingredients associated with protection magic. Some of the most commonly used protective herbs include angelica root, allspice, bay leaves, clove oil, eucalyptus leaf, and flower oil, and rosemary herb and oil. Other common ingredients include amethyst gems and crystals such as black obsidian, hematite, and smoky quartz.

Packaging Your Protection Spell

If you are going to try to block negative energy from entering your home or keep manipulative people out of your life, you should plan to cast a spell with all the ingredients listed above. However, people may also want to use protection spells to invite good energy into their lives. For example, you can create a spell that will attract a new friend into your life. To create an invitation spell, you should plan to use ingredients such as a bay leaf, applewood, lemon oil, honeysuckle flowers, carnelian gemstone chips or powder, and jasmine oil. You can also include angelica root in your invitation spell because it is commonly used for this type of magic.

Choosing Your Protection Spell

Before you perform any kind of protection spell, it is important to understand that protection spells can be used in different ways. You may want to protect yourself from negative energy or other people who might be trying to manipulate you. Protection spells can also be used to increase your overall protection and block out negative energy from the people around you.

When performing protection spells, you should always start with an invocation to the gods. This will ensure that your spell is cast correctly and that good energy is brought into your life. The next step of any protection spell is to create an altar that will include all the ingredients you plan to use in your spell. You can then light a candle and offer libations to the gods to establish contact with them. Once you have established contact, you will be in a better position to cast the spell in a way that will allow good energy to come into your life.

When performing a protection spell, you should always consider the type of protection you are trying to achieve. Some people may need to protect themselves from negative energy or manipulative people around them. Others may want to block out negative energy from the people around them or be protected against manipulative people.

Protection spells should be used in moderation. If you constantly rely on protective spells to avoid negative energy, it can become easy for people trying to manipulate you to affect you negatively. Before performing a protection spell, it is important to consider the effects of this type of magic and whether or not you will be able to block out negative energy from your life without using a spell.

A Protection Spell for Beginners

This is a simple protection spell that you can cast without following an exact recipe. Before you perform this spell, it is important to create an altar that will include all the ingredients you plan to use, such as salt, sandalwood, bamboo leaves, and a piece of hematite. You should then light a white candle and use it to draw in positive energy. Once you make contact with the gods, perform the spell by moving your hands in a clockwise motion and drawing energy into yourself.

You can then use this positive energy to protect yourself and block out the negative energy trying to come into your life. This type of protection spell can be used on its own or in conjunction with other types of spells you want to cast. You can also use this spell if you are struggling with negative energy from manipulative people or trying to block out negative energy from the people around you.

Protection Spell for Psychic Protection

If you are constantly struggling with negative energy, it is important to perform a psychic protection spell. A basic psychic protection spell should include black tourmaline, kyanite, quartz crystal, and rosemary leaves. You can also include angelica root in your psychic protection spell because it is commonly used for this type of magic.

Before you cast your psychic protection spell, it is important to create an altar that will include all the ingredients you plan to use. You should then light a black candle and use it to draw in the appropriate type of energy. Once you make contact with the gods, you should move your hands in a clockwise motion while reciting an incantation. This will help you to create a psychic barrier that will block out negative energy from your life and protect you against manipulative people who might be trying to affect you.

Performing a White Light Protection Spell

White light spells are a great way to protect yourself from negative energy, manipulative people, or negative energy that comes from other people. To perform a white light protection spell, you will need to create an altar and include all of your ingredients, such as pure water, white flowers, quartz crystals, and Angelica root.

Before you perform your white light protection spell, you should light a white candle and use it to draw positive energy. Once you make contact with the gods, move your hands in a clockwise motion and chant an incantation, such as "I am under the protection of the light" three times.

You should then take this positive energy and push it out of your body to create a white light protection spell around you. Although this type of protection spell will not harm negative energy, it is designed to push this type of energy in the opposite direction. Negative energy will be unable to pass through your white light protection spell, which will help you feel safe and secure.

It is important to remember that magic energy is powerful and can cause problems if it is not used correctly. Before you begin practicing any type of protection magic, you should remember that this is delicate energy that must be handled in the right way. If you are not careful, you can hurt yourself or other people in your life. When practicing any type of protection magic, it is important to make sure that the energy moves in a clockwise motion to help build up the psychic barrier. If you do not turn your hand in a clockwise motion, it can cause damage to the barrier and weaken your protection spell.

Conclusion

This book has presented you with information on how to use the phases of the moon to draw magic into your life. Now, we will summarize our findings and offer suggestions on how you can continue to enhance your magic. The first chapter contained spells to help you connect to your intuition for future spells. Each of the following chapters included several spells and rituals, all of which were based upon the phases of the moon. There are several ways to continue developing your craft, and you should consider them all. It is not our intention to limit your growth but rather to help you find new directions and paths of magic.

The following are some suggestions on the best ways to expand your knowledge of the phases of the moon and further develop your craft:

First, you should find a teacher. Many people have successfully developed their craft over the years, and any reputable teacher would be happy to offer guidance. A good teacher will help you develop your skills, connect you with students of a similar level, and will help you stay on track. As long as they have a good track record of positive feedback, it doesn't matter whether you find a teacher online or offline.

When you have a strong foundation in magic and have found a reliable teacher, you can begin to focus on your interests. The first three chapters of this book helped you hone your intuition and gave you what magic would be most helpful for. For example, if you have a strong interest in astrology, you should begin exploring astrology and the planets associated with the moon.

If you enjoy the craft and want to make a career out of it, you can attend college. There are many colleges for witchcraft, and you can even attend online classes if you wish. There are also many available books on the subject at your local bookstore.

If you have already been practicing magic for a while now, you might consider hosting a group of students. Not only will this expand your craft and fulfill your need for a community, but it will also help you earn additional income. It can be rewarding to teach others and see them develop their craft in the same way you did.

Now that we have summarized our material and offered suggestions on how to continue growing, we should take a moment to thank you for reading our book. We hope that it helps open doors for your magic and eventually lead to additional opportunities. The knowledge provided will give a great foundation for building a successful career or achieving personal enrichment. If you wish to continue growing, then great! We hope that whatever direction your magic takes leads to happiness and plenty of adventures!

References

Ahlquist, D. (2002). Moon spells: How to use the phases of the moon to get what you want. Adams Media Corporation.

Guardian staff reporter. (2000, October 28). The witching hour. The Guardian. https://www.theguardian.com/theguardian/2000/oct/28/weekend7.weekend3

Herstik, G. (2021, April 22). These Full Moon rituals are actually magick. Cosmopolitan. https://www.cosmopolitan.com/lifestyle/a36200187/full-moon-ritual/

La Pompe-Moore, G. (n.d.). How I finally nailed mindfulness, thanks to the moon. Byrdie. Retrieved from https://www.byrdie.com/moon-rituals

Moon, C. (2021, January 10). Witchcraft Moon Magic Spells by Chalice Moon. Waterstones.Com. https://www.waterstones.com/book/witchcraft-moon-magic-spells/chalice-moon//9781801474245

Moon magic: A beginner's guide to learn lunar spells and rituals for witchcraft practitioners. Use moon energies to boost your wicc (paperback). (n.d.). Rjjulia.Com. Retrieved from https://www.rjjulia.com/book/9781801093507

Thomas, S. S. (2018, July 3). How to harness the magical power of each moon phase. Allure. https://www.allure.com/story/moon-phases-magic-spells

Wicca Moon Magic: The wiccan guide to perform Moon Magic. A witchcraft grimoire for learning and practicing Moon rituals using spiritual (hardcover). (n.d.). Elliottbaybook.Com. Retrieved from https://www.elliottbaybook.com/book/9781914024153

Witchcraft moon magic spells: A grimoire and Wiccan guide to exploit the phases of the moon to perform magic works and use lunar energies for master (paperback). (n.d.). Boswellbooks.Com. Retrieved from https://www.boswellbooks.com/book/9781801474245

Witchcraft moon spells : Guide for Wiccan beginners willing to study and perform magic spells based on lunar characteristics. Discover mysteries like Witches of ancient times. (Paperback). (n.d.). Walmart.Com. Retrieved from https://www.walmart.com/ip/Witchcraft-moon-spells-Guide-Wiccan-beginners-willing-study-perform-magic-based-lunar-characteristics-Discover-mysteries-like-Witches-ancient-times-P-9798624920606/744667679